# OLD HAT

# OLD / HAT /

ROB / WINGER

NIGHTWOOD EDITIONS

2014

Nightwood Editions
P.O. Box 1779
Gibsons, BC V0N 1V0
Canada
www.nightwoodeditions.com

TYPOGRAPHY & COVER DESIGN: Carleton Wilson

Nightwood Editions acknowledges financial support from the Government of Canada through the Canada Book Fund and the Canada Council for the Arts, and from the Province of British Columbia through the British Columbia Arts Council and the Book Publisher's Tax Credit.

This book has been produced on 100% post-consumer recycled, ancient-forest-free paper, processed chlorine-free and printed with vegetable-based dyes.

Printed and bound in Canada.

LIBRARY AND ARCHIVES CANADA CATALOGUING IN PUBLICATION

Winger, Rob, 1974-, author
Old hat / Rob Winger.

Poems.
ISBN 978-0-88971-296-6 (pbk.)

I. Title.

PS8645.I5725O43 2014 C811'.6 C2014-900622-5

*Everything happens again and it's never the same.*

– Ethel Wilson as Nell Severence

## CONTENTS

## RE/SIGNS FROM THE BIG BOARD

Press operator for zero.
Press menu for pound.
Please try your hang-up and call again.

Do not arm raises.
Do not intersect blockage.
Do not drink your drives.
Do not attempt to defeat the polarization
of your plugged-safe attachment purpose.

Exit emergencies only.
No red on rights.
Enter donut.

Workers doubled when speed fines present.
Use of prohibition motorized.
Drawn ahead: caution bridge.

The Fox expressed here does not represent the opinion of views.

Persecutors will be violated.
Performers may be strip-searched.
Suggestive parenting is strongly guided.
This is an open door, never keep fired.

Board on, baby.
Come on to yielding traffickers.
Bump speed ahead.
John 16:3.

Please inform your pregnancy if you suspect you are a doctor.
Please keep excessive minimums to a noise.

Smoking no please.

If you have a nurse, please give it to your x-ray.

Please keep your personal longings with you at all times.

At the dash of the long end, followed by six seconds of silence,
the clock will be one.

It's the know of the world as we end it.

# SET

## AUTOMATIC TRIPLE-X FIREWORK JESUS

Out past the sunlit-pine median and Georgian coast,
scrubbed white sky shows us where the ocean is.

Both Carolinas are Cracker Barrel Bingo cards;
we stop at every McDonald's for pee breaks

then leave the interstate, shuffle past real-life
bright-orange chain gangs wrestling ragweed,

patched asphalt turned to rivers by speakeasy thunderheads
outside Savannah, all the perfect alley cats nestling

into flowerpots. Over the bridge, the trees get greener;
the Spanish moss extends, *Fireworks!* billboards

multiply, a hundred white redeemers picketing pornshops.
South, south, past Ray Charles' anthems into the static

alligator swamp between here and Key West,
our shelling left to a screened-in Gulf Coast balcony

then rebuilt into blue-line daydreams.
Every Smoky Mountain pass we pilot, later,

rolling all the way to Canada, is already
a *Road Atlas* away from Disneyworld.

In this barnacled seashell rests every road we took.
If you put it to your ear: the truck stops.

## WHAT WE THOUGHT

*after Matthew Zapruder*

You put on the first album you ever bought
and the pastel map turns dusty.
Remember that margin where the song
dips down into silence? Can that take us

to the Sunday School basement, where Judas or Peter dies,
so they lay his felt effigy sideways on the green board
and raise triumphant above their pinkish hands a radiant
red-headed Christ? (None of them have heard of Palestine.)

Next door, the country-mile railroad leads to shows:
a visiting Methodist choir; a visiting Presbyterian missionary;
a visiting troupe of men in cork, their olde-tyme stump speeches
unsure how creaking clippers got retired from the sea.

It's best to understand we were just kids. That we built dangerous
forts out of bent Plexiglas, climbed green quarry walls,
trudged over nuclear-waste mountains to school every morning
and only ever knew Cowboys and Indians.

The genteel townsfolk still used the word "negro" then.
We lumped it in with all our other translations for "foreigner."
Wayne Gretzky had grown up next door, and damn, he was *Polish*,
we thought; not a single one of us knew Grant Fuhr wasn't German.

In that Alice Munro story, written before we were born,
they cram into the crumbling town hall to stare at the black Africans
and wring their hands with pleasure when they sing so "authentically."
Somewhere in 1979, that's happening in small-town Ontario;

it might be still. We were made to read their stories, though not as if
they mattered. Our fathers worked with them, lowering steel into
the underworld of smelters. They called them strong but didn't elaborate.
How we've ever found the names for things I'll never know.

Somewhere, I ride my first thirty-three-and-a-third RPMS
down the angry Appalachians all the way
to the muddy south, where the needle hits its vinyl edge,
then goes to sleep in its silent, salted cradle.

## SOUTHERN ONTARIO STEREOSCOPE

i.

This here's gingerbread.
I cut it down from the porch myself,
before it burnt, I mean.

Don't know why. But it's kept all these years.
I kept it all these years with my tools.
This here got mouldy, though, out in the shed last spring.

A drip somewhere. This was my farm.
The swimming hole's down by the CN line.
That (a ditch) is where the hobos would come to work.

They'd sleep in our loft. The greatest invention?
Electricity, that was quite a thing. TV.
Maybe the party-line telephone.

No. The tractor, I guess. The tractor.
Right where that mall's being built:
that was the front porch, with the gingerbread.

And this, the Beer Store: that was the main house.
That lot there was the school,
and that ball diamond was corn.

That there was Mac's; he'd bury his money sometimes
under fence posts. Pull in here, would you?
Now this. This here was the old town hall.

ii.

At the great water, so-called, downhill and still,
you might find arrowheads, fieldstone graves,
a shingle, a milk bottle from the thirties.

The so-called great water was witness
to all that frontier claptrap, stubbornly glimmering
against the same old shore. A mile of ice, even.

Palimpsest, stone hammer, scratched-up country chalkboard:
we're listening. Our rubber and tarmac and plastic
could be levelled by one strong breeze.

What did the water whisper before General Motors
or Darlington, before the Centre or the rink
or the hydro lines cut your acreage to bits?

Stand in the field and put out your arms.
Below the concrete, earth. Below the earth, an aquifer.
Grab onto your divining rod. It's almost gone.

## IDI TSE-TUNG

He has never seen the sea, never mountains.
He has never turned a wheel, riveted a hull,
pulled a trigger, trained a telescope.
He has never held an oboe.

He has never entered mineshafts,
never worn lipstick or wigs.
He has never crushed a skull or a grasshopper,
never weaved a burlap sack for kittens.

Across the beehive, more workers.
He's never talked to them.
Across the pitch, there are armies in the valley.

Across the homespun rice paddy
or Burmese jungle-clearings,
shining blades from Europe.
He's never met their makers.

Their Pepsi-bottle mothers couldn't help.
Their fathers were spunk leftover
then abandoned in spittoons.
Every last sibling was a folded lawnchair.

He has never held a passport,
never scaled an armistice,
never watched a port catch fire.

The tea in the cup, the oracle hissing,
the mouldy matchmaker stinking up the lintel:
he has never plucked a basket from the Nile,
then wiped it clean with reeds.

If there are fissures in the windshield,
they spread each winter.
Wet paint on the benches, the guardrails gone,
the last plate clean and ready for the next.

The final word
of every film
is almost always fine.

Nothing's ever started with a single, simple tick.

## LAMENT FOR LONESOME GEORGE

Beyond the kitchen, solar flares
turn rooftops to genome maps.
There are tidal pools in the dishwasher.
Sink-spoon newlyweds teethe
on one another's factory labels.
Satellites draw vectors for streetlamps.

Nothing is predicated on anything.

Except, maybe, for the squirrels, risking roadways
for winter nuts. Or the fridge, where polar caps
endanger asparagus, and Freon fracking shudders
the freezer's mantle. Tomato cans rust.
Shuttered clothes-dryers declare their sexuality.
Every lost bolt is a caged tortoise.

How many species were discovered in 1972?

There's no answer we can believe in.
Phil Esposito in 1972: "We're in a war, man,"
a bad haiku pulled whole from headlines,
every cutlass wrecked or pickled,
every cloud: a bored ocean.
That weird dude on the sidewalk could be your dad.

No matter what they pay, you're lonely.

So every teenage feeling is Keats all over again.
With all your unhatched, x-rayed eggs,
they stuff and ship you home to Darwin.
The microwave's particulate soaks our countertops,
our plastic trash cans hidden behind pressboard.
Our linoleum thunderheads won't break

until we turn our strawberries into cardinals.

## MEAN DEMOCRAT, NICE REPUBLICAN

i.

Pretty dirty gulls skirt the grocery store parkette;
they make no bones about wanting bread.

You can depend on the wind, you say
– or they do.

Out past the shallows, there are tiny swells.
The shoreline, as predicted, is summer green.

But everyone likes that; they say either *So!* or *So what?*
There's cellophane all over the cattails.

Up against the picnic bench, two high school kids
push their tongues into each other;

our knees are too old for that.

Every time I ride my silver bike into town,
the sky presents itself in mystery-novel prose.

ii.

On my phone, I track a long-dead satellite, designed
to map our oceans, still circling its fruitless longitude.

The porch is dark with rooftops;
our spines curl into bookshelves.

The weeds, in the dark yards, waiting for whackers,
grow their flowers anyhow.

## YOUR FATHER'S TEMPER

Your father's temper is a woolly iron,
an expected black kettle,
the bite of a barb in a worn-out worm.

Your father's temple is a well-struck cutter,
a full-hewn timber,
an open office for Champlain's astrolabe.

Your father's timer is a fractured fist,
cocked against Gyprock or collar,
blows and bruises and busted seams.

Your father's timbre is a one-two punchline;
if you write it, okay – he'll still
plough the corn into diamonds.

## THE LIGHT BRIGADE (REDUX)

This fall, a three-year-old black
bear turns from tamarack
to north campus undergrad.

*Fuck Tennyson*, he's thinking,
or maybe Hegel, stooping through
plastic litter or snooping

into first-year psychology textbooks,
with their boisterous, self-evident graphs
and overinflated new-edition barcodes.

The river continues to sit still and move.
Across the quad, new beams embrace
the bridge's mid-century-modern arches.

The sandbox cedars root into banks
too broken to hold deposits.
There's nowhere else to go.

What will his paw leave behind
with his tidy turds and berries,
his fervent initials ripped into birch bark,

all the grey classrooms leaning
against any old forest,
where every wild animal's still winter?

In the woods, even the trees are true.

## GIVE ME BACK MY MUSE,
## YOU FINGER LICKIN' BASTARD

I keep track of my place in your book
with a Jari Kurri all-star card, flawless,
not even a crease in its three-decades-old corners.

In place of your birth year are square brackets.
In place of maple leaves or a crisp shirt-and-tie selfie,
two hot rock stars flank your cowboy-hat Telecaster.

I'm sitting at the cultural crossroads of Oshawa, Ontario:
an abandoned Starbuck's, near the mall.
Torontonians complain that it's minus five in January.

Bundled kids in Prada jackets
trundle through the drained reflecting pool,
texting friends about Jessica Alba's baby.

They signed Yu Darvish without seeing his fork.
They signed their books without looking up at us.
They gave you fries with that without even asking.

I'd like to say the campus inspired. That the already-dated
million-dollar classrooms shone. And I'd like my ten bucks
back from the back-lot parking attendant, please.

But, by the time I started my earnest limericks on English horses
and Persian syrup, you'd already mastered
the Zen professor's infernal coconut machines.

What's the point, I think, over a Tall Breakfast Blend,
of trying to live up to that? I've turned into Mr. Furley.
Still too dumb to notice Jack's great, big, throbbing zipper.

## ANOTHER LAKE POEM

This lake's not deep. Its sludge
gathers with dumb muskies
at the bottom, unbeautiful to everyone.

The land does this or that sort of slope-y
thing, the ditch sumac all red and drippy.
The water ripples and sits there;

all the animals are small
and brown; all the loons
are leaving for America.

The lovely sun simply means
we can't stop cutting the grass just yet,
our gorgeous leaves erased by lit gasoline.

Inside the municipal library,
a brand-new window cuts the water
into five skinny rectangles.

Canoes rust under beech trees.
At least I think they're beech.
They're near the beach.

Soon, snowmobiles will cut desire lines into the lake.
Dopey winter fish will pace the angry drones
they've heard about from slimy grandfathers.

I'm six feet above the earth,
blocked by hidden, pinkish insulation;
these windows aren't metaphors.

If I took out the nearest boat
and peered intently over that old,
instinctive edge, though,

I'm guessing
the reflection there
might tell me something new.

# RE/SET

## RE/LENT, WITHOUT CHOCOLATE

How to do it
without roses, mourn

without Kleenex, protest
without precious medals,

hope without that selfsame Icarus
and his tired goddamned wax.

Here are the woods: axes
and thrushes, ferns and frost.

Here, the sea: the sad Atlantic's slave holds,
the angry Pacific's coral Crusoes,

and the sky's ad nauseam Soviet satellites
spelling out their milky limericks.

In the infield, white men lay out.
In the library, women mean it.

Put down your pencils and nubby rubbers.
there's no detour around this traffic jam;

we'll turn on the air
and wait.

## RE/COVERING CHAMPLAIN TRAILS

All poems must include the following:

our singular gift for discovering spring:
the signature tulips, slush-grey clouds, inflatable
metaphors over lookouts, overlooking the Canadian

Club bottles littering the constructed escarpment we figure
as virgin, leaving interpretive plaques and other tourists
out, and our reluctant, ecstatic withdrawal from the sublime;

how we trace the national (Anglo-)Canadian Shield
with bushed mantras on lumberjacks on invented
fossils, on tiny, historic Frenchmen who ate sea turtles,

one-dimensional wildlife bursting into our special conditions
of postmodernity: bearclaw cherry tree, beaver dam,
sugarbush woodpeckers, golden hawks gloating

in the turgid updraft, and our plucking of the first
red trilliums from the syrupy undergrowth
with a triumphant squeeze of pliers;

the apex, where we edit out a flawless man-made
bench, cut a tattered copy of *The Idiot*:
diction dimmed, pages drenched, spine reeking fungus;

the apex, where we gaze deeply into distant
Holsteins scattered over hot checkerboard vistas
and omit their patties from our songs of pure forest,

of solitary genius, of the man of feeling,
of the dazzling, bolded sky we bludgeon into terza rima
with every Arcadian method for clearing ground;

a penultimate plastic umbrella for our
brimful saccharine goblet and one last punchline
on lacklustre cedar, say, or everyday wind,

on distant shelling or mirrored lakes or deep-sea
blues, on every precious flower crushed beneath
our chic two-hundred-dollar soles.

## RE/ACHING FOR THE EIGHTEENTH CENTURY, OR RE/ALMS FOR THE POOR

The hill-tribe poem, the leper poem:
pre-postcard, pre-currency;

the muddy slope where our four-hundred-dollar
backpacks recline, the guide unpaid.

Here's where we compare spiritual affluence
and national roughage,

where kids are undamaged
by suburbia or higher thought,

where the doctor who left and doesn't write home
is the problem,

where the Pamela Anderson pin-up posters
are quaint misunderstandings,

where blood-baked circumcision stitches stay uncounted,
those thirteen-year-old HIV-positive girls

stuck into albums to defend semi-annual,
tax-free donations to UNICEF.

We have words for coffee, for trees for bears for love,
but nothing for the whole, authentic village

watching Archie Bunker reruns
on the Sabbath.

The stilt house funded by the city pimp
isn't translated.

We say the hookers *wanted* service, the beer bottle willingly wound up
bobbing solo in the surf, the maid didn't deserve a tip, anyhow.

Our farmhands, with their hand-woven baskets,
will never have time for Christopher Lloyd's flux capacitor.

Everybody's guilty of arrival.

## RE/MARKS ON THE CENSUS

i.

Ankle-deep in mothballed archives
we discover genetics,

each ship's festering hold stuffed
with expectant storyboards:

syllables drip from armed customs officers;
someone clears the hardwoods;

spiles are turned into trunks;
the pure earth, harnessed with hand-hewn pitchforks.

The New World rapes of grandmothers
that means our blood is mixed.

ii.

On our Walpole Township crop farm,
my great-great-grandpa Abraham is still
a Tunkard drunkard, no matter how you slice it.

His body is tied to the same horse
every Saturday night at the Hagersville Hotel
then carried ten concessions home

beneath Orion's holey shield.
Every ship: a second
arrival.

## ROMEO RE/ACTOR RE/MEMBERS THE BODY

We've got neck napes, jewels, Joy Division
pull-quotes,

but outside there's always sunshine
twittering pussywillow blooms.

We're nude not naked, loving not horny,
pure but unpredictable;

we put our palms on a breast
and declare human rights,

put our tongues on a nipple
and slug down formula.

At the climax, we're still the sash
in a weighted window.

We thrust a jigsaw into the drywall
and cut out a new bay.

Screw blueprints, we say,
going off the board.

Love conquers awl.

## RE/MORSE CODE RE/QUIRES COMING LOOSE

i.

At six, new drones are launched
by or at this or that faction;

we watch their flak jacket sunlight
emasculate the word *Press*.

A new father cradles his son's
headless torso astride the anchor's potholes,

our swimmer's itch rubbed clean
with Freon-rich local lotion.

ii.

Some memories can only take shape decades later,
forgotten first and then remembered

as burst bullets, not trauma,
not capital Freudian baloney,

just stars, poplars, thumbs across a tabletop,
that pattern in an aunt's linoleum.

The pad on this TV remote as tender
as a newborn robin.

iii.

After reading Wilfred Owen, say, or screening *Schindler's List,*
the point is to turn trench-foot

into the empty skulls of *Halo 4*, to put head-patting lectures
on the 1940s into quaint context.

If we realize our aunts were sexy in their day
or why uncles stayed home with the winter wheat,

maybe we can also include these intestines,
knifed out (just yesterday)

into a Baghdad gutter, stuck between
two static Iwo Jima radios

and the cool foxtrot of our idiot
Western Front.

## RE/EVES AND ADAMS

i.

For best results, frame specific kids
against desert backdrop, say,
or slo-mo mortar fire,
standing for, epitomizing
the body's gospels.

ii.

In the Gatineau river: a Mohawk prostitute;
in Edmonton suburbs: made-up girls and wrung wives;
in an East Hastings crackhouse, a Jarvis Street dumpster;
in a Halifax port, already lost when the container's pried open;
in Brampton, Mississauga, Etobicoke, Pickering,
with every frosty fence;
in rural high school washrooms and lunch lines;
in Winnipeg slums with triggers;
in Inuvik glue cans, Ottawa think-tanks, St. John's hulls,
Cape Breton manses, neon Montreal jazz joints;
in Quebec language laws; in Saskatoon scarves;
in bright-lit Banff bedrooms, where we wax and wane;
upriver, underwater, below the mountain, above the valley;
the bread in the kitchen; the bikinis on CNN;
the strippers you paid to perfect your baldness;
locker-room punchlines, the grass cut just so;
the woman at the toy store, scolding boys in pink;
the man on the golf course with his blue-leather GPS;
on Scarborough's bluffs, in Calgary's oily calculus,
along the dull border's illusions: they're right here, soldiers.

iii.

We should know this by now.

Put that chivalrous sword back
into its dull, little scabbard.

iv.

Yes, this is *that* one, with witness.
Put up your dukes and quote Leviticus.

Here's the mantra where we lament federal majorities,
blindly striking out the plates we're spinning.

If we give you an open palm, you'll slash it
into trees.

This is the one where our strophes rise up
against the Westerlies.

So what if we rip that election sign
in two?

v.

The fingers are male, the ones that plant bruises;
that put them on the desk and hike up their skirts;
that ask them to join the meeting with sugar and cream,
that *tsk-tsk* military enlistments, that put out their eyes
with battery acid, that drape them in doctrinal heat
or pious blue, that scratch them notches for innocence,
marriage, motherhood, demure disappearance;
that drown them in the canal in the name of whatever.

Men still fill the streets,
in charge
and possible.

vi.

Old Britannia and Lady Liberty,
Queen Victoria and Hurricane Katrina.
April, May, June, July. Wednesday.

Pillars don't excuse their arches.

vii.

Put your callused palms, if you've got them,
into the owned earth.

Live up
to your biceps.

Curl your
dumbbells.

Shuffle your office
into clarity.

If you have factory light,
if you have brotherhood,

if you have cigars or fishing hooks
or paternal instinct, let it simmer.

Your forefathers
beat them.

Your mortgage-free whiteness
isn't providence.

None of us walks out of here
unless we all do.

# LECT

✦

# (PROGRESSIVE POEMS)

## SIDDHARTHA BY THE RIVER, FOR YOU (REDUX)

After ten years on the shelf, we lose

the plot line, the anchor, the dénouement of stillness,
resolve to back and fill

in something specific about a river ferry
about a palace, something in the offing
about the certain indiscretion of leaving.

We jury-rig the wilted spine, and the river's there,
continuing, and we want old Hermann to be even-keeled
and flawless, the simplest cosmologies we read
in the whole nine yards of any Penguin paperback;

but, Govinda, you son of a gun, why are you still
following that barefoot hermit's buckets of fog –
cold enough to freeze the balls off a brass monkey –
when what we really need's a respite from that old asceticism,
from what holds water, what still makes a high-water mark

from our retired currents? When what we really want
is to make headway, to skylark without going by the board,
three sheets to the wind, and only the devil to be paid
by some P.O.S.H. naiveté that takes the wind out of
our sails, that hauls up short our failing deadlights, takes our
mainstays down a peg, stem to stern, the intake valves of memory.

## “THE MIRROR STAGE”

is a title bearing transcendent ideological resemblances to Foucaultian / Derridean / Kristevan philosophies of the phallus of power, of onion skins and state apparatuses (central to the functioning of the post-Weimar American wings of the Frankfurt school), meaning we might assume (barring interpellated, Simmel-induced frenzy or "estrangement" of the crowd's circumstantial megalomaniacal tendency towards pre-structuralist flaneur-ist transgression within individual subjectivities) that vamps are reviled objects of desire, as Kristeva had it (and as Rich postponed it or Butler's performativity made manifest), whilst tramps are the admirably alienated superstructural subjects of production set within a neo-Marxist ideology separated from its signifier (formed by its *own* second-order signification and driven, as such, by Barthes' pedestrian Citroën) in order (following Harvey) to be co-opted by the spatial practices inherent in any return to the Freudian principles of pleasure-sexuality-death (i.e. the mirror stage and the Wolfman), and ultimately become, via now disproved meta-narratives of domination and absolution, trauma and flashback, the *female* inversion of Bhabha's mimic men (emasculated, et cetera), the post-coital, postcolonial post-productions of Sontag's campy/kitschy inevitability centered on the simulacra of contemporary, hybridized transcultural identity crises so prevalent within post-human figurations of fusion and messianic symbologies of meaning as to be a problematic *qua qua qua qua a propos* of varied, positivist postcard intimations of naively mono-critical dialectics. Or, to clarify, they simplify the synchronic reading practices of duality and binary opposition within a prefigured, normative, post-structuralist, contemporary heterosexuality: (the words are the same except for their openings.)

## U-BEND, BREAKER

*Always go better than code.*
– Mike Holmes

What we've got here isn't just your basic blockage; it may be a feed line or a copper, likely. Here. We'll try PVC because of the chlorine. It's impervious. Not white, though, and not PEX or brass fittings. That's for suckers. The stack's just fine, so that's a relief, and all your ABS and HVAC look good. We won't be dealing with off-gassing VOCs, either. Thank god they did the Tyvek right! These fittings look like R-2000, but, good god, you've still got knob and tube in this wall! At least your service panel's where it should be. I'll open things up down there and have a look. Let me put in this GFCI first, though; it's wet, and we sure don't want to arc to your belt buckle! See now, we're still hot here; maybe your AFCI's gone; it's not tripping. Have you had many shorts? Your junction boxes are all messed up; maybe that's it. Here, you've got twenty-five amps running on both these breakers; that's not right. And this one's only roughed-in; and there's more tubes in these studs, too! No wonder your loads are high! Your box can't run for path of least resistance because it's channelled, see, so you can't put 3,000 watts into every switch; that's just asking for a fire. They're not even grounded! Let's start with the wiring, then the pipes. We'll run extra ABS to fish future wires through, and use the old joist tubes for a start; at least they're level. I'll get you a new box and put in more GFCI's near your wet outlets. We'll solder the copper for now, but we really ought to overhaul everything with Ipex, if you want it right. New valves will let the stack stay put, so we'll ditch the old lead toilet tie-ins, too. Sound good?

## DETECTIVE FICTION

*Army Dad Loses taste for revenge in Iraq*
– news headline, March 2006

About the grid.

About Cheesecake Factory slices spilled
on Scotchgard upholstery.

About the Xeroxed, dry-walled, trailer-park utopia perched
on the porcelain fringes of power lines, fallow fields, city.
About who's right and who's dirt.

About how accountants treat the waitress, the *Sun*, pharmacists' salaries.
About the four-bedroom depravities of having no pool, no cable, no time:
the old, brown-shoe baloney that's McCarthyism dressed up
as eight-point *fuck you*s coming from a car horn.

Sweatshop T-shirts and Volvos and Halliburton parentage aside,
suburban bodies still need water and light, still have the heart for,
are at the heart of, break hearts over the right stories
in the right mouths; the tender for the fire,
the bass beneath the soloist.

So, let's get this straight: the hooked trout is desperate and almost dead.
Pigs and cattle are meat, not pork, not beef, not friendly, overdressed
vegetables. The dark is frightening and full of unwanted entries.
The abstract debris in the sewer grate still defines what's possible,
our Mississauga children testing love at the confluence of oil leaks
and flowers, of pearly used condoms and all our crispy dandelions.

## OLD HEMINGWAY DEVOTEE

*Write me a poem,* she said, all red roses.

*If you want the West Wind,* he said,
*stay in the parlour.*

This was the nineties, when naming was big.
We burned women as wolves, in effigy, then.
*I'll write you a poem,* he said, *all about toilets.*

She cracked open his jaw with one well-paced *Fuck you.*
*If this were a real war,* he said (once she'd left),
*the men would be nuts cause the women are anvils.*
The waitress' icepack was stuck to his check

and the old-timers turned to the pitch and the call.
*Write me a poem* he sang out to Clemens,
as he snuck in a strike past the lead-off man's beer gut.
The man at the warning track useless as dirt,
TV's blue bleachers still stitched to my shirt.

## PAVANE

A solidbluelineonthefloor guards the triptych's stained glass

moths, oak metronomes, clapper teeth, foreshortened chopsticks:
dance steps on the sixteenth century's floorboards.

If you lean over the line, you'll find shadows,
the happenstance of records made in single afternoons,
credited on their brittle sleeves as three vinyl hours

on specific, long-gone dates.
The granite security guard keeps tabs on distance,
the possibility I'll smoosh fifty years of oil.
*The artist,* he says, closing in, *was terribly arthritic*

*by 1954, you know; he laid himself down*
*on raised platforms to ease his back pain – just so! –*
*and painted with a little French trowel, hence this smear,*
he says, pointing. He's been standing for hours.
A Jersey lyricist's Breugel, here we have the most express

abstractions of abstract expressionism, the Automatiste mood
manifest and epitomized, not quite calligraphic (as in later work),
not quite écriture (as earlier), but epigrammic, perhaps,
primordially landscaped, receding and advancing
as though natural light, organically connected to voyageurism,
created these raking diagonals of its own accord.

Someone stuck the blue line to the floor.
Someone stretched and framed the cloth.
Someone cleaned up the edges and typed the label.
Someone decided which category was which,
which *which* to include on his dusty c.v.,
which mosaic meant money.
This is not an apple.

## HEDGE FUND (REDUX)

Suzy's got three and Johnny's got two.

Henry's got four and Jane's got the dirt.
A seed for an apple, but Suzy wants two.

*Okay, one for one,* she says, but Johnny's
got ears. And Jane, on the ground,
holds up stones with her skirt.

*If one seed's one apple,* she says, with aplomb,
*let's say one rock means one pencil, so two*
*are just two, and three mean one of each.*
Johnny gets four stones. Suzy gets three.

Henry goes one for one, and Jane keeps accounts.
*If a pencil's a stone,* she says, *and two pencils an apple,*
*how many to get your shirts and blue mittens?*
Henry wants mittens now, and Jane, Suzy's blouse.
Johnny trades apples and soon has no socks.

*Listen,* says Suzy, *you can return them with harvest,*
*but you'll have to give extra – I'm in love with their lustre.*
Jane says, *If five stones equal two boots, and six are one shirt,*
*I'll give you all apples for laces and collars.*
No one sees the pencils now (it's far too close to lunch),
they all sell their socks at cost to feed their groaning guts.

Jane, in shining shirts and boots, is none the worse for wear.
Suzy's ledger starts to bleed and Henry's in despair.
*Give me stones or give me naught,* he says, sounding like a dolt.
He's only had one apple slice, and for that he paid four stones.
Near the dirt, where Jane began, the pebbles calmly rest.
If pencils mean warm underwear,
then winter must be best.

## ANOTHER BIRCH ACROSS MAIN STREET

The birch across the street is October yellow

but its bark is no *Homage to a Square.*
It's still bare, frosted, lit, beauty, et cetera;

still present, framed conveniently
in a rented, diamond-cut window
and we'll still walk by and hear it, later,

still remarking on the space
between twigs and wind.
We'll hang our mantras
on its busted branches

and call it a paintbrush
for white, rain-glazed chickens.
We'll tell anyone listening we were there
and felt something, will disconnect a *radif,*
an apostrophe, a beat, on purpose.

Remember: the failure of that telling isn't the tree,
isn't just a word smuggled into *street.*
Remember: if you turn down the hall
for another cup of coffee,
all your yellow photocopies
will get smudged.

Outside, greater primaries will spread
and secondary coverts will open;
scapular swoops will power those mantles,
all their orbital rings shielded by brilliant
gonydeal angles and supraloral foreheads.
Welcome, you'll think, to the cognitive classes,
where all the old lines lead directly to dinosaurs.

# SET

## LAMENT FOR RUBE WADDELL

We misread you, hayseed. All those times the fire trucks pulled you from the diamond, mid-windup, you were chasing Blake.

Colonel, Pirate, Cub; Orphan, Athletic, Brown: the spoons and puppies they held aloft to throw you off (your flutterball left hanging for cleanup) were every cure for Moloch.

Your whole first signing bonus blown on a single whisky binge, they fined you fifty bucks for drunkenness, so you disappeared for months, to Canada, then showed up at the circus, *bam!*, wrestling Florida alligators.

You forgot how many women you'd married (there were three), twirled batons astride parades, played fullback in California, rugby in hometown Pennsylvania, soccer in St. Louis (all for cash).

You showed up sauced and started anyhow, late from marathon marbles matches with random homeless sinners, then vanished for weeks, walking into the 1905 pennant race, mid-inning, holding up a catfish for your manager.

"A million dollar body and a two-cent head," you claim to have learned your craft by "throwin' rocks at birds," changed into uniforms while streaking from left-field beer parlours, and never wore underwear.

You denied that hundred-dollar fine for a "hotel episode in Detroit" by shouting, with vigour, "You're a liar! There ain't no Hotel Episode in Detroit!" then carried your loaded pistol into road motels, where it once went off, brushing flat the bushy eyebrows of Connie Mack.

In 1900: a seventeen-inning win followed by a same-day doubleheader shutout, egged on by your coach's promise of a free three-day fishing trip you never got. Is that justice, Rube?

July 1, 1902: the first time anyone ever had an inning with nine strikes and no balls.

You rescued men and boys and drowning logs from frigid rivers, starred in the vaudeville flop, *The Stain of Guilt*, ad-libbing all your lines because you couldn't remember them.

In 1903: 302 strikeouts. In 1904: 349. You iced your arm for hours, fearing, with fierce sincerity, that you'd tear a hole in the catcher's mitt.

What did they whisper when you followed Honus Wagner into Pittsburgh, the century dumping its dirty luggage on all our Platonic porters?

"Nusty," they called you, without love, not yet drunk enough to pass out on that 1909 New York mound.

That twenty-inning game you won against Cy Young, then sold the game ball for beer.

It was Doc Powers who waved everyone off the field that time so you could fan the side, Rube, solo. But we shouldn't judge; every other time it was you who sat the boys behind you, on the infield, high on crumbs or bourbon, as you retired everyone and sighed.

193 and 143. Your first game thrown at the same age Jesus met his maker. Four twenty-win seasons. Your two-title triple crowns, fifty shutouts, 2,316 strikeouts. Put into the hall two years after the war was done.

In Hickman, Kentucky, you sandbagged a broken dike for thirteen hours, frozen and penniless and up to your chest in sludge, until the frost etched curlicues into your lungs.

You died – a lowdown southpaw – in a Texas TB sanatorium on April Fool's Day, 1914, thirty-seven, younger than I am now, still quick, sold to the 1908 St. Louis Browns for five thousand sorry bills.

## DEPARTURE LOUNGE

The coffee's shit, and the company greasy,
but the sun dazzles the bookshop,
our forty-eight-hour deodorizers failing,
the blank security barriers

with their bludgeons, uniforms and lunch bags.
Two decades back, we'd all be smoking.
But now, sunsets play out behind clean glass, one-hour WiFi,
all our novels thrust into designer carry-ons,

and the merciful phones-off runway rules,
so our bodies end where the gates begin,
each fuselage hosting
a complex grand-staff of silence.

In two hours, you'll be in Kabul Korea Connecticut;
last calls, standbys, a sloppy seatmate's missed
connections, the sure slope of the plane
down the grey ramp

past newspapers and perky pleasantries,
until they seal behind you
every step you might have taken
with every flight illuminated on the grand, black board.

Were there similar ascents
when the ocean meant gales and doldrums,
the docks that knew the seas' names
dreaming New York against dirty, concrete channels?

Buckle up. Leaf through the creased magazine.
Here's the captain's creed.
Your shoulder against the window, an inch from stratosphere.
The green earth down there will soon be mooring thunder.

## THREE LITTLE PIGS

*after the shelter in* Walden

1.

It was inevitable: that puff, this wreckage. I'm the oldest, after all. I crept up from the Neolithic goo and fastened my instincts to straw, against my mother's wishes. I pulled twine from my brow and tied it to structure. My father grew up in the mud, so this was a step up. I munched myself into architecture long before Orwell. My grass gathering was the granddaddy of agriculture. That dog that ran it over was as thoughtful as a meteor.

2.

They say my kid brother's the smartest, but I just got bad luck. Who needs the goddamned pen when we've got these here woods to chop down? That's what *I* did. And it would have worked if it weren't for the damned earth giving way. Oh, I sharpened those sticks! I've seen me some history and I know full well what happens when they overrun the whatever – the castle walls. I shoved each stick into the ground. Tiger traps, they call them. Sure, I used mud to jam them in. But that's neither here nor there. I've gotten past mud and straw. Just come on back any day and try that again. I'm headed out and you better be ready. There it is.

3.

I could never settle on plains, in dirt, across open pens, under rain. I held a stethoscope to a cliff wall (and that was tough; my legs are short) and the granite called back, I swear. Right here, I told my brother, right here is where the ice age started. This charcoal crack's a glacier, see? He didn't say much, and the other one told me to hush up that bullshit. That's just how he said it. But I pushed a wheelbarrow through the Great Wall of China anyhow, and I set myself inside. Everyone knows they both ended up here, too. I'm not proud; that's civilization. The way that wolf slowed down into a wheeze was the first fast food chain. Here, at the hearth, in the den, under the high-raised roofbeams, finally, when the stew was simmering and the first lamps lit with gold, the time was ripe for Jesus.

## CELLPHONE

I'm explaining to my class that no one knows
anything about anything.

Truth is a tortoise photographed
in the seventies, I say, or, as one guy puts it

from the back row, the only thing for sure is that
"I do and/or do not exist," stressing his oblique.

There's no Walt Whitman, I'm saying, up there,
in a respectable shirt made in Bangladesh,

unless we all agree that the milk in the glass
from the cow is the farmhand.

Outside, the sky continues its meaninglessness.
The potted plants don't bother to lament.

Heels sink into lawns and airplanes become algorithms
for the deep weight of heavy water.

There are espressos digging in
beyond the lectern's bored cement.

Everyone, I'm saying now, eats the carrot root
and throws away the flowers.

Nothing I say is ever ready
for reason.

## SOMEDAY I WILL LIVE IN BROOKLYN

but not on 1980s iron-fence Dumbo side streets,
language like raspberries blooming
from fiery Italianate brownstones.

I will ride lettered trains to Manhattan,
where the toy store will be choc-a-bloc full
in its old, crumbling location,

the Park all manner of safety, even the moonlit
Sheep Meadow, even if Prospect's better.
Someday, I'll hop the turnstile home

to Brooklyn, before the stainless steel future
arrives with sealed thunderclouds
and other post-CGI clichés.

My son will still be eight and noble;
winter Sakura will cover the lawns.
Someday, I will live in Brooklyn,

but without its cool French patisseries
or desperate little berets
or bagel shop lynchings.

The sea won't be far.
There will still be bridges.
The gleaming Midtown needles

won't be Gotham, but atonement,
clean and sleek as a can
of Diet Sprite.

## OCCUPATION ISLAND

i.

In the *Post*, court injunctions rub shoulders
with the new American League MVP,
our first pitcher in a quarter century.
Is he the 1%?

Should I tweet doctored versions of that orange
cop with UC Berkeley pepper spray or maybe
the one dressed like Martin Scorsese, who crossed
the pride line to avoid betraying his brethren?

Soon, all the pretty celebrities will get divorced
and face us at the checkout, where we buy chips
processed in Iowa. In the cooler, all the colas
will be hot red. The cashier will press a foot pedal

to bring forward our selections. What will we do
with our clever jokes about Beat poets,
out west, where the sun still is?
Weather means nothing in the subway.

ii.

The yuppies are starting to feel uncomfortable.
Way back, that was them at the reflecting pools –
they had guitars and bugs and knew
which sign to hold up when.

They're here with us now, drinking
fine, dry cappuccinos in one-horse small-town
eco-shops, where everything's organic.
And this foam? Well, it's delicious.

(The cavemen in Lascaux wore skins
they'd made themselves.
I wish they'd come forward
to smack us with their fine-boned clubs.)

## PASCAL'S WAGER

> *You'll never see a horseshoe making a blacksmith.*
> *You'll never see a pot making a potter.*
> – Daniel Dennett

Pulling tight against his blue duvet, my kid's afraid of bedtime robbers.
*They'll come in the window,* he says. *They've broken into cars*
*in people's driveways – I heard you guys.*

We're buried in a small-town basement bedroom.
I tell him the thieves are fictional. *Focus on what's good,* I say.
In the corners, crumpled jeans morph into claws.

I say that out there, there are wars and fires.
Some kids starve, can't read, wait for bombs, live in dirt shacks.
Parents manage fear, I say, and I'll carry his, okay?

On the TV upstairs, a walrus-shaped American tells another
just to love his wife. He's a doctor.
There's no mention of tanks or lesbian existence.

No mention of right-wing primary candidates
quoting the Book of Revelation
or pharmaceutical sales or Marx or purdah.

No talk of America the Great Satan
or Osama Bin Laden's sons or the production
of Agent Orange in small-town Ontario frying pan factories.

Were these Jurassic limestone fossils planted (as tests) by Jesus,
I could ask. Can the weasel frog's elbow prove irreducible complexity?
Is your necklace a bit of the true cross or ark

or ark of the covenant, or is all that just Indiana Jones?
*But I'm afraid,* he says. Under the covers,
clutching a plush penguin, he takes another breath.

The books on my shelves keep quiet.
*That's for real,* one of us says
to the other.

## THE OPENING SHOT OF *MANUFACTURED LANDSCAPES*

It's possible to think furrows can't waver,
that the gleaming apples on the witchy bough,
dusted in milky pesticide, are perpetual perennials,

that all the trees fell from space
and buried their knotty heads in the earth,
that all the buildings are made of Lego.

Unconstructed: the sky,
some of the lakes, the waterfalls
we haven't dammed.

Unconstructed: drumlins and boulders
and silt left as glacial markers
(unless you've got religion).

Below the surface of the lawn,
all the grubs, devils, caverns
and mines are made up.

The gasoline in our cars comes from Esso's buried tanks.
The food on the shelf was never grown.
The mail arrives only because we think it might.

Through the window,
the fictional world takes stock.
I haven't built it any more than you have.

## SEPTEMBER STILL

Across the erstwhile diary duck-fog,
we're still. Stairs spin into long-lost
slingback benches, our lit, backdeck
hibachi, rusted through to dreck.

They say the emerald-headed ducks are migratory,
which means they depart and arrive responsibly,
cutting into weeks of still water as though
moored in deep hypnosis psychotherapy.

Beyond our proletariat essays, vines still ripen and pop.
All the stones become blackbirds.
We stop-down so light can flood our frames
with the greatest possible depth of field.

No river stays as frozen as these ducks do.
The water beneath the steeples in that photo
you took on the park boardwalk, still using film,
fifteen, maybe twenty years ago,

greedily young, all our grandparents still alive,
our hairlines and budgets not yet receding.
The past is a country closed by revolution,
entered only by sunset, every staid September.

# RE/SET

## IN ADDITION TO REFERENCING RE/FUGEES, AND OTHER BANDS,

this next poem is roughly based on two historical figures
whose scientific methodologies are clinically tied
to a summer I spent at an asylum, now boarded up,
by Lake Specific, where the yellow paint,
I was thinking, when I wrote this next poem,
concerns a central myth of the French Revolution,
regarding Marie Antoinette not actually saying
that famous cake thing, which I read as a theory
of how poetry can alter the consciousness of John Keats,
something that needs to be understood
before I read this next poem.

What I was trying to do, when I wrote this next poem,
was consider those characters and their rejected theories,
which deserve a few minutes of explanation
before I read this next poem.

Their at-first derivative analyses of the newly discovered
Element X was only recognized as genius in retrospect,
once they were long dead, like Van Gogh,
whom I'll remind you about for a minute or two
before I read this next poem.

One died of syphilis, which had such-and-such
an infection rate in so-and-so a country during
whatever detailed period of history I'm now referencing,
and the other grew older and older (relying on a hand-carved cane
that appears in the penultimate line of this next poem,
made from cherrywood, whose molecular structure figures

in this next poem's final lines, and which I'll explain in a minute);
and the other was run over – the second scientist, I mean –
by a wagon whose wheels were made of the same Element X
whose subatomic strength made it possible
to fuse entropy theories with lay understandings
of the actual physics that informs any sort of expert
knowledge of the foundational geometry
I've admittedly butchered in order to structure this next poem;
so pay no attention to the actual mathematics I've
just loosely alluded to when you listen to this next poem.

To really understand this next poem's connection
to Marie Antoinette, you need to know about Napoleon's time
in Corsica, a time with which you may already be familiar,
but which I'll still detail to ensure you can understand
the way lines seven and eight dovetail with my implied conclusions
regarding both the physical scientists who originally
discovered Element X – here are *their* names – and the
historically connected events that similarly inform the maybe
made-up bread shortages of eighteenth-century Paris
to which I allude in this next poem.

Now, let me say a little something about structure.

In this next poem, all of the even lines do this, with historical examples,
except for this one, which is unique owing to the influence of this surrealist,
French linguist whose very interesting biography I'll now briefly sketch
so you can appreciate where that exception comes from in this next poem.

The odd lines are "free," but only in the theoretical sense
I'll now summarize with the following exegesis,
but which I won't belabour in the interest of time.

Rhymes and metrics go like this and this
for that and those reasons and, it might be helpful to know,
before I read this next poem, first, that my iambic leniency
is due to this or that detailed manifesto regarding
the revolutionary sound poetics of this capitalized,
named-after-the-fact socio-artistic movement and its proponents,
all of whom I'll name, now, for you; and, second,
that the suffragette movement in southern France
figures prominently in the strophic whatever of the
particular syllabic whosits throughout the following whatnots.

Finally, when listening to this next poem, it's useful to know
that my parents were both penitentiary librarians and that I, myself,
was once convicted, and spent a night in the very prison
where they worked so hard for their whole so-so lives.
The arrest was for tax evasion, hence the Willie Nelson lyrics
scattered throughout this next poem, except one phrase,
towards the beginning, that actually comes from
the Pet Shop Boys, believe it or not;
here's that quotation, in full.

I won't say much more for fear I'll bore you to death
with all the cane-work details.

Here's the poem.

## RE/WORKING THE ASSEMBLY LINE

Just last week, a two-inch spike ricocheted off the concrete floor
into the neck of a man four years from retirement.

Gun-jockeys sweat sunshine
into the mustard boards of forklifts,

punch clocks bound for container ships,
crates and plastics assembled, later, elsewhere,

used once
then thrown into dumpsters.

They bust or heroize the union, depending.
Bylaws come and go. Sorry, no change.

Lime-coated foul-line diamonds.
Tanned lifeguards who never apply their training.

Garbage incinerators
nestling a great lake's armpit.

Chickens coated in their own shit, processed
by hands paid per snapped neck.

How far is it from here
to the lemonade stand?

## RE/CALLING ALL ICARUSES, COME IN ICARUSES!

i.

Deep as the (inevitable) ocean
here's the one where the toilet becomes Icarus

where the tax collector is Icarus
where our attempts to woo bodies between sheets are Icarus

where the mud puddle's dull rings are Icarus
where Icarus is peanut butter, or mucus, or your own mother.

ii.

Why devolve into feathers when bay bridges are what's right,
here, where bagged kittens sink into un-beautiful deaths?

And Icarus, the dumb-ass, is nowhere near romance:
he's a cautionary tale for parents of unruly accountants,

his body one of three elliptical dots
preceding our monochrome quotations.

## RE/TREATING LAMARCK'S THEORY AS MY OWN GRANDPARENTS

1. and 2.

My grandfather's cedar. His stink,
six hours into milling. His hammer.

Or his wife's diabetic chesterfield
below the white Jesus print.

How her protestant skirt rises towards a dangerous panty line
where two grey folds of skin flank the bypass staples.

> *Here,* she might've said, *hands took out a blood tube*
> *to stitch into my heart in three clean loops.*

Here's her rail line crosshatch, her creosote thighs;
dry riverbed, *jouissance.*

3. and 4.

My grandmother never wanted news.
Just hockey-town boxscores. The crosswords.

Her apse filled up with local politics and pancake Tuesdays,
she sang soprano Sundays, always in her recliner with a book.

Years after he died, she could hear his long-gone car
arriving each midnight,

could still recite her own mom's instructions
for the flakiest possible crust.

Her husband's hospital clichés: shadowy cheekbones,
open robes, lemony skin and that death rattle. .

Here's how his fingers excised photos from shelves
on ever-whisky birthdays, weaving facts over what was lost there.

*That's me,* he said, just that once,
*The first one on the right.*

## ROAD RE/SIGNED

> *I have been stupid in a poem.*
> *I will not alter the poem*
> *but let the stupidity remain permanent*
> *as the trees are*
> – Al Purdy

I drive north to get back to the land-
scape poem, to test the *real-life* hypothesis.

The heart-cross-guardrail combo makes me blubber into muskeg;
fences and used John Deere lots rust into sonnets;
all the remaining silos need paint.

The dusty-gold, government-plaque pioneers
patch their stovepipe pants before the roads are built.
I don't follow their concessions.

That cluster of pine stumps might be what I'm looking for.
How long did it take to dig them out of the clay
into a smudged, ten-second effigy?

Could "Escarpment Blues" and fair-trade
Yirgacheffe really be enough to square our pages?

All the stems of Queen Anne's Lace
are rigor-mortis caterpillars;
the gnarled trees clutch dramatically.

Pine-tree islands, adrift among crop lines,
turn full-on Zen in retrospect,
but the frozen fields will never be Passchendaele.

Forget conjecture. Pointillism gets me exactly nowhere.
Lift me out of these boxes, gearshift,
and sing yourself all stupid, now.

## RE/WARDS AND PRIVATE ROOMS

Sure, there could be falcons,
holy black bears heading underground,
or that wet-nosed baby deer, checking out winter
traffic on the cramped Don Valley exit ramp,

but we pick the old dog,
the one greyed and limping,
en route to the park, sniffing for excitement
despite her sad, dyspeptic bowels.

The mange-ridden, three-legged scamp
we used to feed rice to,
whose soft little puppies all
died in a concrete stairwell;

or those treasured, yappy
shih tzus put to sleep
and how we tried to explain it all
to the angry, adoring kids.

In the deep bits, there's leviathan;
in the shallows, sunlit, jellyfish stingers,
our dads reading the paper
on the beach and our moms,

bless them, insisting on cover-up.
Out in the river, char and salmon and the like,
with their swollen stories of return,
but back home, we prefer the rusty old cat

sitting patiently by her dirty, porcelain dish,
waiting all morning, say, in one arthritic pose
for that last delicious spoonful
of grainy, processed goo.

## RE/CESS POOL, BE KIND, RE/WIND

*every built thing has its unmeant purpose*
– Adrienne Rich

We scoop the snow into a boy-sized bowl.
January, so ice strips stripe the fenced acreage.
There's a forest across the field, empty.
And an unseen factory, built into abandoned
1940s air hangars, still labelled with pre-Helvetica serifs.

In the bowl, earmuffs mute every clichéd whisper.
The wind passes over a fine, blue afternoon.
We're all alone in there, and safe, other boys
drifting down sheets, only to be kicked in the balls
by girls already angry with lipstick.

We're all snow white save one poor Sikh kid
and all the Indians. All of us are up in arms
when they christen those queer United preachers.
The fort walls are as thick as our chests were.
If you get in, your only choice is to squat.

When the bell sounds in maybe 1984, we stay put
at the bottom, frostbite-free, all that golden sun,
our K-mart snowpants still pristine, the last minstrel show's
final frumpy stump speech. Everyone, we know, is filing into lines.
It's now or never, kid. Get up and cross that whiteout.

## RE/PAIR BEATS HIGH KING

To formally resist a new foot
and maybe confirm it, too,
we dip French forks into the AGO's
nouveau-riche fondue pots,
imported faucets hidden
by the fogged-up front staircase.

Later, Japanese knives
slit our conversations
into hundred-dollar grills,
an onion tower shoots up steam.
*It's a volcano,* the chef explains.
It is.

Your grandfather's poplar windbreak,
planted during Civil Rights, outlives him.
It tells us we've all failed
to follow procedures.
We click down the platform,
still humming the same Blue Rodeo.

*All kinds of trains,* you say,
*are ready to arrive.*

## ACKNOWLEDGEMENTS

Earlier versions of some of these poems appeared (or will appear) in the following: *Arc, Contemporary Verse 2, Event, Geist, Hazlitt, In/Words, IV Lounge Nights, The Literary Review of Canada, modomnoc, Ottawater, The Peter F. Yacht Club* and *Public Poetics*. Thanks to all the respective editors.

"Southern Ontario Stereoscope" is for Fred Puckrin (in memoriam); "Give Me Back My Muse, You Finger Lickin' Bastard" is for Dave McGimpsey; "Pascal's Wager" is for Davis – you're the best, bud; "Siddhartha By The River, for You (Redux)," "September Still," and "Re/Pair Beats High King" are for Kristal, with love.

The epigraph from Ethel Wilson comes from *Swamp Angel*. The inspiration for "What We Thought," and one of its lines, more or less, comes from Matthew Zapruder's "Poem for Jim Zorn" in *Come On All You Ghosts* (thanks, Matthew!). A phrase from Samuel Beckett's *Waiting for Godot* appears in "The Mirror Stage." Technical terms and the epigraph in "U-Bend, Breaker" come from Mike Holmes' 2006 DIY guide, *Make It Right*; special thanks to brother John for checking my wiring. "Pavane" is based in part on the painting by Jean-Paul Riopelle, held at the National Gallery of Canada. Avian terms at the end of "Another Birch Across Main Street" come from *The Sibley Guide to Bird Life & Behaviour*. The opening line of "Departure Lounge" is modelled on the opening line of David O'Meara's "Station" in *Noble Gas, Penny Black* (thanks, Dave!). "Three Little Pigs" responds to Thoreau's *Walden*. Many thanks to Albert for the line quoted in "Cellphone." "The Opening Shot of *Manufactured Landscapes*" responds to Jennifer Baichwal's 2006 documentary on Edward Burtynsky. The epigraph for "Pascal's Wager" is quoted in *The God Delusion*, by Richard Dawkins. The epigraph for "Road Re/Signed" is from Al Purdy's "Trees at the

Arctic Circle" in *North of Summer*; "Escarpment Blues" is from Sarah Harmer's 2005 album, *I'm A Mountain*. The epigraph for "Re/Cess Pool, Be Kind, Re/Wind" is from Adrienne Rich's poem "Powers of Recuperation" in *Tonight No Poetry Will Serve*. Thanks to all.

Hearty, incredulous thanks to the Ontario Arts Council, Canada Council for the Arts and *Arc Poetry Magazine*'s poet-in-residence program. There's no way this book would have gotten done without your help.

Thanks also to Brad Cran for the Vancouver 125 Poetry Conference, where I found new heroes; and to Silas White, Carleton Wilson and the Nightwood team for faith and confidence.

Special thanks to those writers and editors who provided insight, friendship and encouragement while completing this book, especially Arthur Motyer (in memoriam), Dionne Brand, Triny Finlay, Matthew Holmes, Michael Holmes, Deanna Kruger, Anita Lahey, David McGimpsey, Motoyuki Shibata, Meg Taylor, Lorraine York and Matthew Zapruder. Thanks, too, to Emily Schultz for her generous phrasing.

David O'Meara and Matthew Tierney: superlative praise and gratitude for your fine, careful, heart-crushing red ink! To Kevin Connolly, with reverence and respect: thanks so much for making this book so much better than it would have been without you.

Finally, thanks to my family, especially Kristal and Davis – who just keep on getting better – and all of our lost grandparents, for every last one of their annual cedar sprigs.

## ABOUT THE AUTHOR

Rob Winger's first book, *Muybridge's Horse*, was a *Globe and Mail* best book, shortlisted for the Governor General's Award, Ottawa Book Award and Trillium Book Award for Poetry, and won a CBC Literary Award. His critically acclaimed second collection was *The Chimney Stone*. Born and raised in small-town Ontario, Rob currently lives in the hills northeast of Toronto, where he teaches at Trent University.

PHOTO BY KRISTAL DAVIS